D1575605

The Artistic Cat

RUNNING PRESS
PHILADELPHIA, PENNSYLVANIA

A Running Press Miniature Edition™
Copyright © 1991 by Running Press. Printed in Hong Kong.
All rights reserved under the Pan-American and
International Copyright Conventions.

Canadian representatives: General Publishing Co., Ltd.,
30 Lesmill Road, Don Mills, Ontario M3B 2T6.
International representatives: Worldwide Media Services, Inc.,
115 East Twenty-third Street, New York, New York 10010.

9 8 7 6 5 4 3 2 1
Digit on the right indicates the number of this printing.

Library of Congress Cataloging-in-Publication Number 91-50613

ISBN 1-56138-091-1

This book may be ordered by mail from the publisher. Please
include $1.00 for postage and handling. *But try your bookstore first!*
Running Press Book Publishers, 125 South Twenty-second Street
Philadelphia, Pennsylvania 19103.

Cats, quite simply, defy explanation. Euclid's geometry can't appraise their curves. Newton's laws of rest and motion fail miserably. Volume isn't constant; even gravity is refuted by a frolicsome feline.

These paragons of grace, paradoxical in nature, are subject to their own laws and heed only their own etiquette. To observe the cat is to witness a singularly surprising creation.

But as indifferent as they are to physical laws, cats have staked a serious claim in the human imagination. Through the centuries they have been worshipped, shunned, and now worshipped again.

*I*n this collection, artists and writers express their affectionate admiration for the mundane yet magnificent house cat. None would be so bold as to presume to solve the mystery of cats' appeal, but each painting and observation may bring us a little closer to the answer.

So celebrate the artistry and artfulness of cats—those kinetic sculptures that bestow warmth even at their coolest. Ever faithful, all-knowing, cats surely have lives that are hidden from us.

Cats are *always* elegant.

· · · ·

JOHN WEITZ
American clothes designer

You see the beauty of the world
Through eyes of unalloyed content,
And in my study chair upcurled,
Move me to pensive wonderment.

I wish I knew your trick of thought,
The perfect balance of your ways;
They seem an inspiration, caught
From other laws in older days.

. . . .

ANONYMOUS

LUCY
Martin Leman

A poet's cat, sedate and grave,
As poet well could wish to have,
Was much addicted to inquire
For nooks, to which she might retire,
And where, secure as mouse in chink,
She might repose, or sit and think.
I know not where she caught the
trick—
Nature perhaps herself had cast her
In such a mould philosophique,
Or else she learn'd it of her master.

. . . .

WILLIAM COWPER
English poet

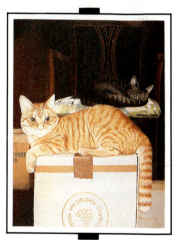

MANGO WITH MOLYNEUX
Joan Freestone

I love cats because I love my home and after a while they become its visible soul.

. . . .

JEAN COCTEAU
French writer and film director

Since each of us is blessed
with only one life, why not live
it with a cat?

. . . .

ROBERT STEARNS
American writer

Cleanliness in the cat world is usually a virtue put above godliness.

. . . .

CARL VAN VECHTEN
American writer

TWO CATS
Franz Marc

Stately, kindly, lordly friend,
Condescend
Here to sit by me, and turn
Glorious eyes that smile and burn,
Golden eyes, love's lustrous meed,
On the golden page I read.

All your wondrous wealth of hair,
Dark and fair,
Silken-shaggy, soft and bright
As the clouds and beams of night,
Pays my reverent hand's caress
Back with friendlier gentleness.

. . . .

ALGERNON SWINBURNE
English poet

CAT
E.B. Watts

$\mathcal{B}$less their little pointed faces and their big, loyal, loving hearts. If a cat did not put a firm paw down now and then, how could his human remain possessed?

• • • •

WINIFRED CARRIERE
American writer

When I'm discouraged, he's empathy incarnate, purring and rubbing to telegraph his dismay...

. . . .

CATHERYN JAKOBSON
American writer

Perhaps it is because cats
do not live by human patterns,
do not fit themselves into prescribed
behavior, that they are so united
to creative people.

· · · ·

ANDRE NORTON
American writer

FELINE PHANTASY
Enid Marx

A cat improves the garden wall
in sunshine, and the hearth
in foul weather. . .

. . . .

JUDITH MERKLE RILEY
American writer

CAT ON A WINDOW SILL
Joan Freestone

There are two means of refuge from the miseries of life: music and cats.

. . . .

ALBERT SCHWEITZER
French physician and philosopher

In these days of tension, human beings can learn a great deal about relaxation from watching a cat, who doesn't just lie down when it is time to rest, but pours his body on the floor and rests in every nerve and muscle.

. . . .

MURRAY ROBINSON
American writer

The cat went here and there
And the moon spun round like a top,
And the nearest kin of the moon,
The creeping cat, looked up.
Black Minnaloushe stared at the moon,
For, wander and wail as he would,
The pure cold light in the sky
Troubled his animal blood.
Minnaloushe runs in the grass
Lifting his delicate feet.
Do you dance, Minnaloushe,
do you dance?

. . . .

WILLIAM BUTLER YEATS
Irish poet and dramatist

Sleepy Cat 3/100   Eileen Mayo

SLEEPY CAT
Eileen Mayo

She moved through the garden
in glory because
She had very long claws at the
end of her paws.
Her neck was arched, her tail was high
A green fire glared in her vivid eye;
And all the Toms, though never so bold
Quailed at the martial Marigold.

• • • •

RICHARD GARNETT
English writer

GOLFING CAT
Hilary Jones

Is it yet another survival of jungle instinct, this hiding away from prying eyes at important times? Or merely a gesture of independence, a challenge to man and his stupid ways?

· · · ·

MICHAEL JOSEPH
English writer

A cat determined not to be found
can fold itself up like a pocket
handkerchief if it wants to.

. . . .

DR. LOUIS J. CAMUTI
American writer

Sometimes he sits at your feet looking into your face with an expression so gentle and caressing that the depth of his gaze startles you. Who can believe that there is no soul behind those luminous eyes!

. . . .

THEOPHILE GAUTIER
French writer and critic

YOUTH
Will Barnet

Mice amused him, but he usually considered them too small game to be taken seriously; I have seen him play for an hour with a mouse and then let him go with a royal condescension.

. . . .

CHARLES DUDLEY WARNER
American editor

BEYOND THE ILEX
Derold Page

How many times have I rested tired eyes on her graceful little body, curled up in a ball and wrapped round with her tail like a parcel...if they are content, their contentment is absolute; and our jaded and wearied spirits find a natural relief in the sight of creatures whose little cups of happiness can so easily be filled to the brim.

. . . .

AGNES REPPLIER
American essayist

You can't look at a sleeping
cat and be tense.

· · · ·

JANE PAULEY
American journalist

To be reminded that one is very much like other members of the animal kingdom is often funny...though...I do not too much mind being somewhat like a cat.

. . . .

JOSEPH WOOD KRUTCH
American writer

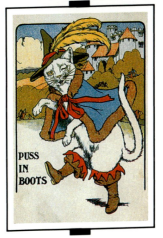

PUSS IN BOOTS
Artist Unknown

. . . **if** you want to be a psychological
novelist and write about human
beings, the best thing you can do
is to keep a pair of cats.

• • • •

ALDOUS HUXLEY
English writer

PENNY BLACK AND TIFFANY TORTOISESHELL
Martin Leman

*W*hat sort of philosophers are we,
who know nothing of the origin
and destiny of cats?

• • • •

HENRY DAVID THOREAU
American writer and naturalist

Like a graceful vase, a cat, even when motionless, seems to flow.

. . . .

GEORGE WILL
American columnist

There's no need for a piece of sculpture in a home that has a cat.

. . . .

WESLEY BATES
American writer

ILLUSTRATION FROM *THE HISTORIE
OF FOURE-FOOTED BEASTES*
Edward Topsell

If there is one spot of sun
spilling onto the floor, a cat
will find it and soak it up.

• • • •

JOAN ASPER McINTOSH
American writer

CAT AND CANARY
Will Barnet

$\mathcal{D}$o you see that kitten chasing so prettily her own tail? If you could look with her eyes, you might see her surrounded with hundreds of figures performing complex dramas, with tragic and comic issues, long conversations, many characters, many ups and downs of fate.

• • • •

RALPH WALDO EMERSON
American writer and poet

I think it would be great to be a cat! You come and go as you please. People always feed and pet you. They don't expect much of you. You can play with them, and when you've had enough, you go away. You can pick and choose who you want to be around. You can't ask for more than that.

. . . .

PATRICIA McPHERSON
American actress

...**C**ats...never strike a pose
that isn't photogenic.

• • • •

LILLIAN JACKSON BRAUN
American writer

SAM, THE ALL AMERICAN CAT
Robert Macaulay

Alexander the Great, Napoleon, and Hitler...were apparently terrified of small felines.... If you want to conquer the world you had better not share even a moment with an animal that refuses to be conquered at any price, by anyone.

. . . .

DESMOND MORRIS
English zoologist and writer

CATS FENCING
Louis Wain

Cats are absolute individuals, with their own ideas about everything, including the people they own.

. . . .

JOHN DINGMAN
American writer

...it is better, under certain circumstances to be a cat than to be a duchess...no duchess of the realm ever had more faithful retainers or half so abject subjects.

....

HELEN M. WINSLOW
American writer

If a fish is the movement of water embodied, given shape, then a cat is a diagram and pattern of subtle air.

· · · ·

DORIS LESSING
English novelist

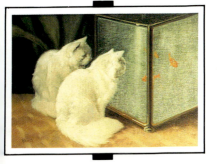

WHITE CATS WATCHING GOLDFISH

Arthur Heyer

Among human beings a cat is merely a cat; among cats a cat is a prowling shadow in a jungle.

• • • •

KAREL CAPEK
Czech journalist and writer

WINSTON AND ANEMONES
Rosalind Stoddart

Thou art the Great Cat, the avenger of the Gods, and the judge of words, and the president of the sovereign chiefs and the governor of the holy Circle; thou art indeed... the Great Cat.

. . . .

Inscription on the royal
tombs at Thebes

The cat keeps his side of the bargain...He will kill mice, and he will be kind to babies when he is in the house, just so long as they do not pull his tail too hard. But when he has done that, and between times, and when the moon gets up and night comes, he is the Cat that walks by himself, and all places are alike to him. Then he goes out to the Wet Wild Woods or up on the Wet Wild Trees or on the Wet Wild Roofs, waving his wild tail and walking by his wild lone.

. . . .

RUDYARD KIPLING
English writer

When I grow up I mean to be
A Lion large and fierce to see.
I'll mew so loud that Cook in fright
Will give me all the cream in sight.
And anyone who dares to say
'Poor Puss' to me will rue the day.
Then having swallowed him I'll creep
Into the Guest Bed Room to sleep.

· · · ·

OLIVER HERFORD
American writer and illustrator

WHO'S THE FAIREST OF THEM ALL?
Frank Paton

A charm of cats is that they seem
to live in a world of their own, just
as much as if it were a real
dimension of space.

• • • •

HARRIET PRESCOTT SPOFFORD
American novelist and poet

A FEAST IN FAIRYLAND
(Jigsaw for Raphael Tuck & Son)
Louis Wain

The cat pretends to sleep that it may see the more clearly....

• • • •
CHATEAUBRIAND
French writer and statesman

You may...if you try hard enough, be able to enter into a very small part of a cat's world...But the world of a kitten is almost impenetrable and you must rest content, mostly, to play the role of spectator. Unless you are tragically handicapped by the lack of any sense of humor you should be able to enjoy yourself.

. . . .

PHILIP BROWN
English writer

■ am the cat of cats. I am
The everlasting cat!
Cunning, and old, and sleek as jam,
The everlasting cat!
I hunt the vermin in the night—
The everlasting cat!
For I see best without the light—
The everlasting cat!

. . . .

WILLIAM BRIGHTY RANDS
British journalist and poet

THREE FRIENDS ON KASAI MAT
Derold Page

Cats speak to poets in their natural
tongue, and something profound
and untamed in us answers.

. . . .
JEAN BURDEN
American writer and editor

PUSSY IN THE WORKBASKET (postcard)
Artist Unknown

$\mathcal{N}$o one can have experienced to
the fullest the true sense of
achievement and satisfaction who has
never pursued and successfully
caught his tail.

• • • •

ROSALIND WELCHER
American writer

The cat does not negotiate
with the mouse.

• • • •

ROBERT K. MASSIE
American writer

A house without a cat, and a well-fed, well-petted, and properly revered cat, may be a perfect house, perhaps but how can it prove its title?

• • • •

MARK TWAIN
American writer

TWO CATS.
Jillian Peccinotti

Wild beasts he created later,
Lions with their paws so furious;
In the image of the lion
Made he kittens small and curious.

• • • •

HEINRICH HEINE
German poet and critic

FELINES AT PLAY
B. B.

The cat has too much spirit to have no heart.

. . . .

ERNEST MENAULT
French writer

Two things are aesthetically perfect in the world—the clock and the cat.

. . . .

EMILE-AUGUST CHARTIER
French philosopher

Lovers most passionate, scholars austere

Both love, when their autumnal

season falls,

Strong, gentle cats, majestic, beautiful

They, too, sit still, and feel the cold

night air.

. . . .

They dream and take the noble attitude

Of sphinxes lazing in   deep solitudes,

Which seem to slumber in an endless

dream.

. . . .

CHARLES BAUDELAIRE
French poet and   critic

WINSOR AND NEWTON
Martin Leman

I saw the most beautiful cat today. It was sitting by the side of the road, its two front feet neatly and graciously together. Then it gravely swished around its tail to completely and snugly encircle itself. It was so *fit* and beautifully neat, that gesture, and so self-satisfied—so complacent.

• • • •

ANNE MORROW LINDBERGH
American aviator and writer

THE FACE AT THE WINDOW
Fannie Moody

If you say 'Hallelujah' to a cat, it will excite no fixed set of fibres in connection with any other set and the cat will exhibit none of the phenomena of consciousness. But if you say 'Me-e-at', the cat will be there in a moment...

. . . .

SAMUEL BUTLER
English writer

Balanchine has trained his cat to perform brilliant *jetés* and *tours en l'air;* he says that at last he has a body worth choreographing for.

· · · ·

BERNARD TAPER
American writer

...**W**hen she walked...she stretched out long and thin like a little tiger, and held her head high to look over the grass as if she were threading the jungle.

. . . .

SARAH ORNE JEWETT
American writer

MINNIE FROM THE OUTSKIRTS
OF THE VILLAGE
R.P. Thrall

She is a sprightly cat, hardly past her youth...she darts out a paw, and begins plucking it and inquiring into the matter, as if it were a challenge to play, or something lively enough to be eaten. What a graceful action of that foot of hers, between delicacy and petulance!—combining something of a thrust out, a beat and a scratch.

. . . .

LEIGH HUNT
English writer and poet

JACK RUSSELL AND PERSIAN
F. Rutherford

*I*f by chance I seated myself to write, she very slyly, very tenderly, seeking protection and caresses, would softly take her place on my knee and follow the comings and goings of my pen—sometimes effacing, with an unintentional stroke of her paw, lines of whose tenor she disapproved.

· · · ·

PIERRE LOTI
French writer

To respect the cat is the beginning
of the aesthetic sense.

. . . .

ERASMUS DARWIN
English physiologist and poet

On some grave business,
soft and slow
Along the garden paths you go
With bold and burning eyes,
Or stand with twitching tail to mark
What starts and rustles in the dark
Among the peonies.

. . . .

A.C. BENSON
English essayist

BLACK CAT
Carole Thomson

He lies there, purring and dreaming, shifting his limbs now and then in an ecstasy of cushioned comfort. He seems the incarnation of everything soft and silky and velvety, without a sharp edge in his composition, a dreamer whose philosophy is sleep and let sleep...

. . . .
SAKI
English writer

THE CHURCH CAT'S DREAM
Derold Page

... one of the ways in which cats show happiness is by sleeping.

. . . .

CLEVELAND AMORY
American writer

Cats are intended to teach us
that not everything in nature
has a function.

• • • •

GARRISON KEILLOR
American humorist and writer

It doesn't do to be sentimental
about cats; the best ones don't
respect you for it...

• • • •

SUSAN HOWATCH
English writer

THE CHAIRMAN
Louis Wain

Some pussies' coats are yellow;
some amber streaked with dark,
No member of the feline race
but has a special mark.
This one has feet with hoarfrost
tipped; that one has tail that curls;
Another's inky hide is striped;
another's decked with pearls.

. . . .
ANONYMOUS

COVEN OF CATS
Janet Thorndike

$\mathcal{I}$t's an honor to paint cats.

. . . .

OLIVER JOHNSON
American artist

LOOK FOR THESE FAVORITE
RUNNING PRESS MINIATURE EDITIONS:

The Little Book of Christmas Carols

The Little Book of Hand Shadows

Love: Quotations from the Heart

Love Sonnets of Shakespeare

Motherhood

The Night Before Christmas

Quotable Women

The Miniature Mother Goose

Tales from the Arabian Nights

Tales of Peter Rabbit

The Velveteen Rabbit

The Wit and Wisdom of Mark Twain

Women's Wit and Wisdom